The Angry Alien

by Kay Brophy

with illustrations by Katy Boys

Copyright © 2017 Kay Brophy

First published in the UK in 2017 by Middle Farm Press
British Library Cataloguing-in-Publication Data
A catalogue record for this book is available from the British Library
ISBN 978-0-9928896-6-1

This edition 2020
3 4 5 6 7 8 9 10

All rights reserved. No part of this book may be reproduced or transmitted in any form or by any means, electronic or mechanical, including photocopying, recording, or by any information retrieval system without written permission of the publisher.

Although every precaution has been taken in the preparation of this book, the publisher and author assume no responsibility for errors or omissions. Neither is any liability assumed for damages resulting from the use of information contained herein.

Published by Middle Farm Press
Author: Kay Brophy
Managing Editor: Kate Taylor
Illustrator: Katy Boys
Designer: Su Richards
Printed by Think Digital Books Ltd

To my friend, Tat

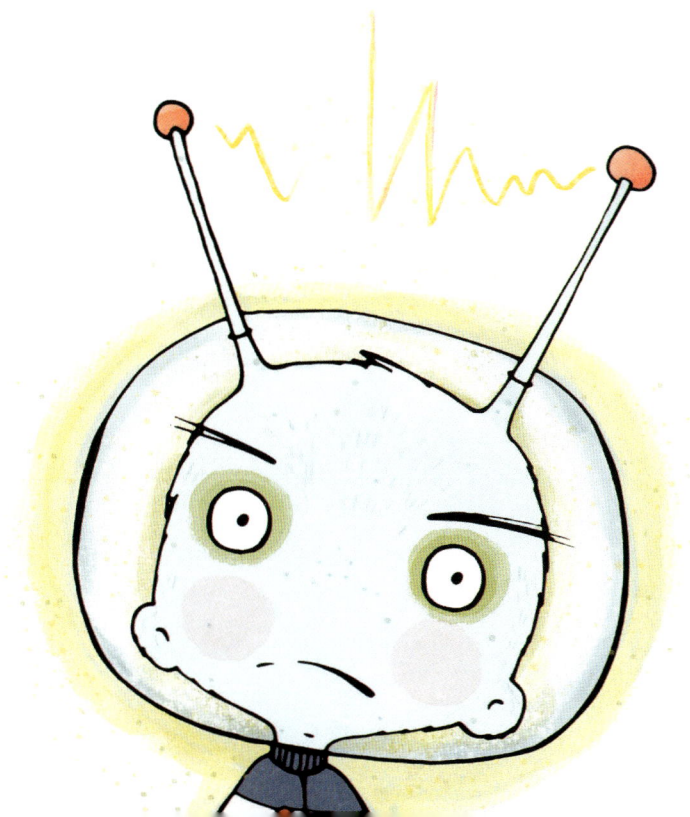

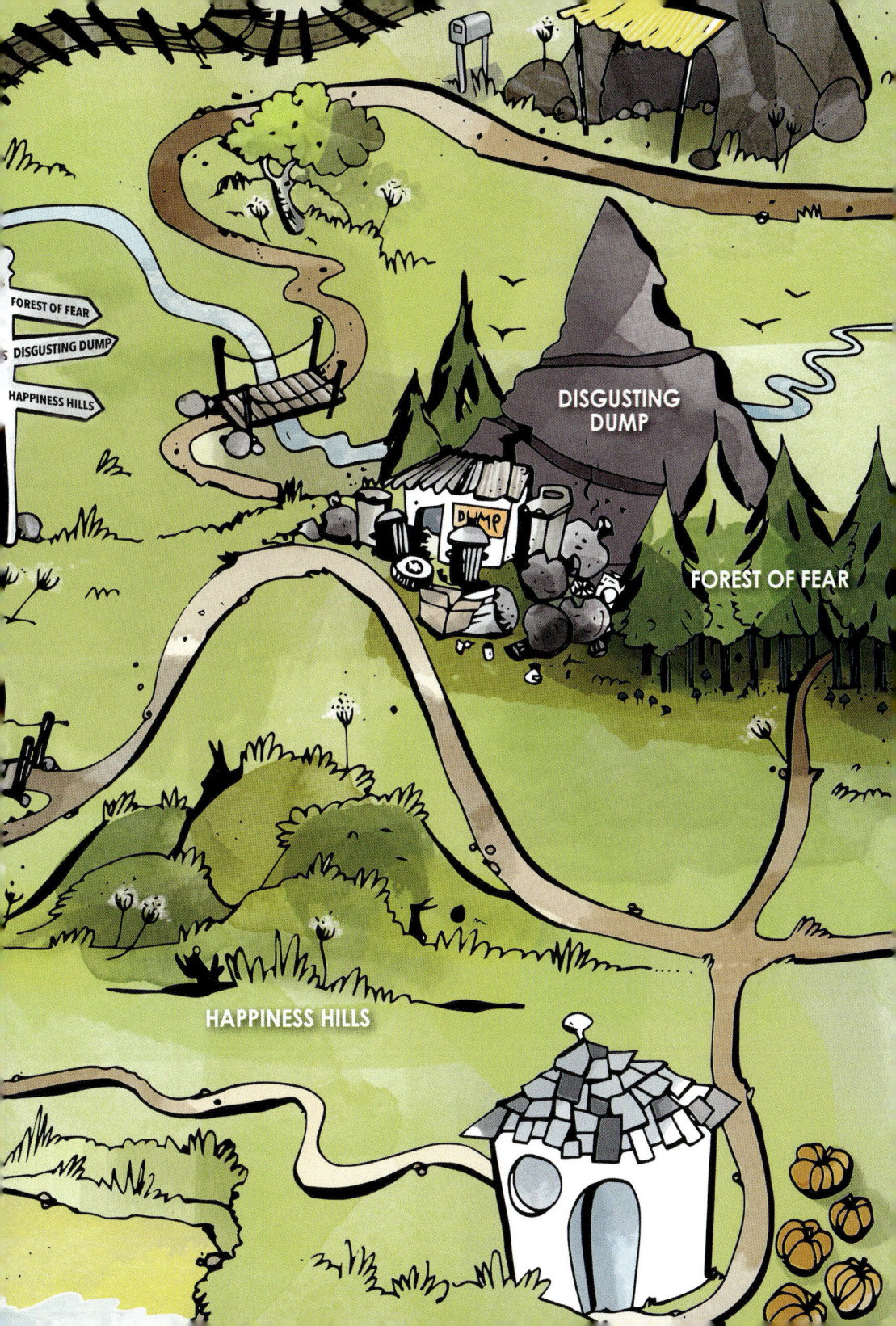

There once lived an alien, so angry and mean
The scariest creature that Lifeland had seen
He wore a strange helmet to cover his head
His angry behaviour filled many with dread

The alien had arrived with an almighty splash
After something went wrong and his spaceship had crashed
He had tried to get home but it just had not happened
So he faced life alone here, angry, abandoned

But one day there came a powerful wave
Which forced Angry Alien out of his cave

Several things had been washed
up onto the shore
Interesting items he'd not seen before

But something was moving
and waving its hand
'Hello! Nice to meet you!
What is this strange land?'

'I'm called Jel by the way, what is your name?'
'Do you want to play? I know a fun game!'

'Get lost!' screamed the alien
'Go home right away!'
'You won't want to stay here,
I have nothing to say!'

Jel was surprised, he seemed sad and alone
'That's fine' she said 'but my shell is my home'

Jel stayed by the cave,
             all day and all night
Alien couldn't believe it when it got light
'She's still here?' he pondered
             'Why hasn't she gone?'
'Maybe she likes me.
             Could I have been wrong?'

'But people NEVER like me;

I hide from them all'

'I make sure they can't see me,

I try to be small'

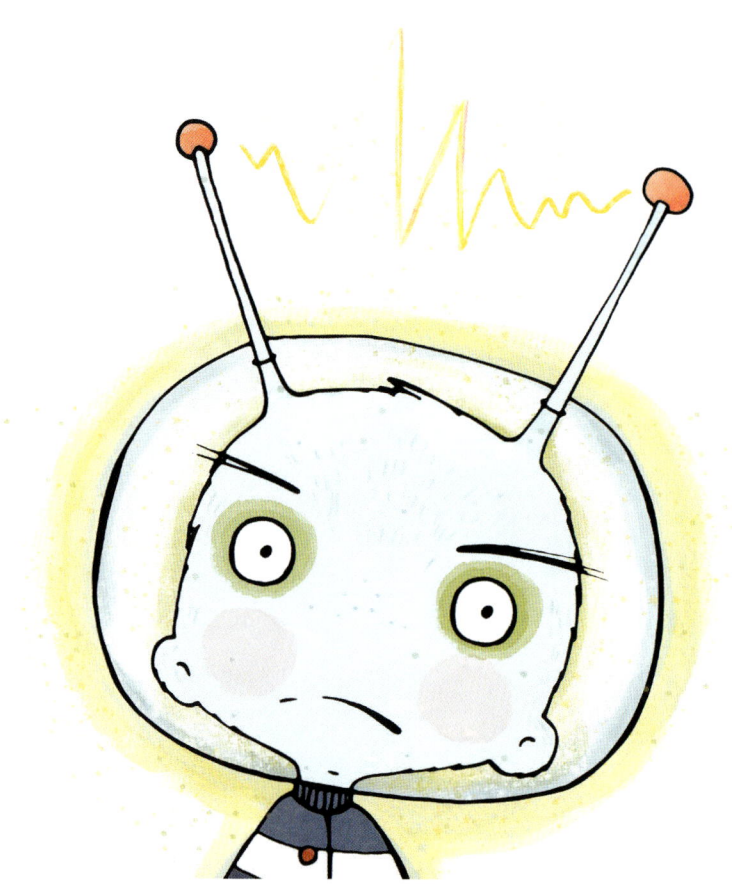

'Is this a trick or a joke you are playing on me?'

'Where is your family?

Go back out to sea!'

'I don't need my family, I'm safe and I'm warm'
'But you seem to be lost in a big 'feelings' storm!'
'I would like to be friends,
can you talk without shouting?'
'If I prove I am loyal, will you stop
all your doubting?'

He thought about Jel and her home in her shell
And realised that he could be happy as well

So the alien and Jel started a friendship that day
And he realised that 'big' feelings CAN go away!

The Angry Alien is struggling to understand his feelings. Join him as he journeys through 'Lifeland', a magical place where he learns about 'big' feelings. Alien meets an unexpected friend along the way, Jel the turtle.

USER GUIDE FOR TEACHERS, PARENTS AND CARERS

All children, in every walk of life, will struggle with their feelings from time to time. The Angry Alien is part of a series of books called Finding Your Way. Each book takes one of the six 'big' feelings of sadness, fear, anger, happiness, surprise and disgust and aims to show the reader how to explore, identify and manage the feeling safely on their own or with the help of an adult.

HOW TO USE THIS BOOK

This book can be read with a child or a group of children at any time. It has been specifically written to help educate children about the feeling of *anger*. Anger is an emotional response to feeling frustrated, blocked or unfairly treated. When we feel anger, we might also feel fear, sadness and/or disgust. Children sometimes find it difficult to talk directly to adults about things that annoy them, they tend to show us in their behaviour instead. So rather than focusing on the child, the adult can help by focusing on how the characters are feeling. For example, by talking about how they think the Alien is feeling when he is unable to get home to his planet, the child will be encouraged to think about their own experiences of anger, helping them to explore these feelings in a safe way. Adults can use the pictures within the book to aid them.

USING THE FIVE Ws

Example questions you could ask while reading this book:

- **W**hy does the Alien need help?
- **W**hat do you think he should do?
- **W**here is he in Lifeland?
- **W**ho helps him to deal with his feelings?
- **W**hen does he feel happy?

Sometimes when children are angry they may also be experiencing other feelings such as fear, sadness, surprise or disgust. Adults can help the child explore these feelings using the 'Lifeland' map at the front of the book. As you read through the book together try to encourage the child to think about where the Alien is on the map. For example, when the Alien is on the beach with Jel you could help them think about where that is on the map, exploring feelings and places together.

Did you know?

- Reading with your child at least four times a week can help them to develop their own reading and literacy skills.
- Talking to your child about feelings can help them develop their emotional language and intelligence.